MONTH OF LOVE

FEBRUARY

MEGHA YADAV

Contents

1. February   1

2. Rose Day   2

3. Purpose   4

4. Choclate   6

5. Teddy Day   8

6. Promise Day   10

7. Hug Day   12

8. Kiss   14

9. Valentine's Day   16

1. February

February, month of love and grace
With shorter days and longer night's embrace
The chill of winter lingers in the air
But the promise of spring is almost there.
Snowflakes dance and twirl with glee
As children laugh and play happily
The muffled sounds of crunching snow
Add to the peaceful ambiance that's aglow.
Cupid's arrows fly through the sky
Making hearts flutter and souls take flight
For in this month, we celebrate
The joy and beauty of love that's great.
February, a time to reflect
On the kindness that we should expect
From those we hold dear to our hearts
And to give love, in its many parts.
So let us cherish this month of love
And hold on to those gifts from above
For the memories made will last a life
And the warmth of love will endure through strife.

2. Rose day

Rose Day, a day of beauty and grace,
A day to show, a smile on our face,
A day to give, a symbol of love,
That speaks more than words, from up above.
For roses are more than just a flower,
They're symbols of love, of joy, and of peace,
They're gentle whispers, in nature's bower,
That bring us closer, and never cease.
With every rose, we show we care,
With every petal, we let them know,
That in this world, they have someone rare,
Who loves them deeply, and will never go.
So let's embrace this special day,
And give a rose, to someone we love,
Let's show them that we're here to stay,
And bring them joy, from up above.
For roses are the language of the heart,
The bond that ties, that never fades,
They're proof that in this world, there's a special part,
That's filled with love, that shines in every shade.
So let us celebrate Rose Day,
With petals soft, and hearts so true,
And let us give a rose, to brighten someone's day,

For this day is a celebration of love, that shines so bright and new.

3. Purpose

Purpose Day, a day to celebrate,
A day to give our hearts a lift,
A day to search and find our way,
And give our lives a meaningful shift.
It's time to ask what we desire,
And set our goals to reach new heights,
It's time to ignite the fire,
And let our purpose guide our sights.
For each of us, it's different still,
Our purpose unique, our paths diverse,
But on this day, we'll find our will,
And chart a course that we'll immerse.
So let's embrace this special time,
And make the most of every hour,
Let's find our purpose, and climb,
Towards a future that's full of power.
For when we find our purpose true,
Our lives will never be the same,
We'll face each day with strength anew,
And conquer all the trials that came.
So let us celebrate Purpose Day,
With joy and hope that never wanes,
And let us find the way,

To live the life that truly sustains.

4. Choclate

Chocolate Day, a day so sweet,
A day to indulge, a day to treat,
A day to savor every bite,
And bask in the joy that it brings tonight.
With every square, so rich and divine,
We'll find a moment of pure delight,
With every taste, so smooth and so fine,
We'll be transported to heaven on sight.
Chocolate is more than just a treat,
It's a feeling, a mood, a state of mind,
A gift that we give and receive,
And a love that we'll cherish, so kind.
So let's embrace this day with glee,
And treat ourselves to a little bit more,
Let's revel in the bliss of thee,
And enjoy every square that we pour.
For chocolate is a simple pleasure,
That brings a smile to every face,
It's a gift beyond measure,
And a joy that we'll never replace.
So let us celebrate Chocolate Day,
With every bite, so rich and divine,
And let us bask in the joy that it brings,

For this day is truly a chocolaty shine.

5. Teddy Day

Teddy Day, a day so dear,

A day to show that special someone, we care,

A day to give a warm embrace,

And show them how much we cherish their grace.

For teddies are more than just a toy,

They're symbols of love, of joy, and of care,

They're constant companions, always with us, to enjoy,

And bring us comfort when we're feeling scared.

With every hug, they wrap us in love,

With every snuggle, they ease our fears,

And with every moment, they're there above,

Bringing us joy, through all the years.

So let's embrace this special day,

And give a teddy to someone we love,

Let's show them that in our hearts they'll always stay,

And bring them a smile, from up above.

For teddies are gifts that truly last,

Reminders of love, that never fade,

And as we hold them close, we're filled with peace at last,

Feeling the comfort, that love has made.

So let us celebrate Teddy Day,

With love, with joy, with a warm embrace,

And let us give a teddy, to show we care,

For this day is a celebration of love's sweet grace

6. Promise Day

Promise Day, a day of trust,
A day to show our love and lust,
A day to make a vow so true,
And show the world, what we'll do.
For promises are more than just words,
They're bonds of love, that we keep,
They're the beating heart of our dreams and hopes,
That help us rise, and never sleep.
With every promise, we show we care,
With every vow, we let them know,
That in this world, they have someone to share,
Their joys, their sorrows, and their woe.
So let's embrace this special day,
And make a promise, to someone we love,
Let's show them that we're here to stay,
And bring them joy, from up above.
For promises are the light that guides,
The path of love, that we all tread,
They're the hope that never hides,
And the strength that helps us spread.
So let us celebrate Promise Day,
With vows of love, that never fade,
And let us make a promise, to brighten someone's way,

For this day is a celebration of love, that's always made.

7. Hug Day

Hug Day, a day to show we care,
A day to wrap our arms and share,
A day to bring comfort, love, and peace,
And offer a warm embrace, that will never cease.
For hugs are gifts that truly heal,
They ease the pain, they make us whole,
They're magic potions, that we all feel,
And bring us joy, that never grows old.
With every squeeze, we show we're here,
With every hold, we let them know,
That in this world, they have someone dear,
Who loves them deeply, and will never go.
So let's embrace this special day,
And give a hug, to someone in need,
Let's show them that we're here to stay,
And bring them comfort, in every deed.
For hugs are universal, and always free,
A gesture of love, that knows no bounds,
They're proof that in this world, there's always a key,
To unlock the happiness, that surrounds.
So let us celebrate Hug Day,
With open arms, and hearts so true,
And let us give a hug, to brighten someone's day,

For this day is a celebration of love, that shines bright through.

• 13 •

8. Kiss

Kiss Day, a day of love and light,
A day to share, a day to unite,
A day to show with just a touch,
The depths of our love, that mean so much.
For kisses are more than just a touch,
They're symbols of love, of joy, and of care,
They're gentle whispers, that say so much,
And bring us closer, in every prayer.
With every kiss, we show we're here,
With every touch, we let them know,
That in this world, they have someone dear,
Who loves them deeply, and will never go.
So let's embrace this special day,
And share a kiss, with someone we love,
Let's show them that we're here to stay,
And bring them joy, from up above.
For kisses are the language of the heart,
The bond that ties, that never fades,
They're proof that in this world, there's a special part,
That's filled with love, that shines in every shade.
So let us celebrate Kiss Day,
With gentle touches, and hearts so true,
And let us share a kiss, to brighten someone's day,

For this day is a celebration of love, that shines bright, so new.

9. Valentine's Day

Valentine's Day, a day of love,
A day to show, what we're made of,
A day to celebrate, with hearts aglow,
The one who makes, our world complete, and grow.
For love is the glue, that holds us tight,
The fire that burns, with a warm embrace,
It's the light that guides us, in the darkest night,
And the happiness, that fills our every space.
With every gift, we show we care,
With every word, we let them know,
That in this world, they have someone rare,
Who loves them deeply, and will never go.
So let's embrace this special day,
And celebrate, with love, and joy, and grace,
Let's show the world, in every way,
The depth of our love, that shines in every face.
For love is the most precious gift,
That we can give, to those we hold so dear,
It's the bond that lifts, and lifts us up,
And the promise that, forever, we'll be near.
So let us celebrate Valentine's Day,
With hearts so full, and love so bright,
And let us show the world, in every way,

The depth of our love, that shines so bright.